Contents

Words shown in the text in bold, **like this**,
are explained in the Glossary.

Who were the Wright Brothers?

Wilbur and Orville Wright were brothers and **inventors**. They **designed** and built the first real aeroplane.

Wilbur (left) was born in 1867. Orville (right) was born in 1871.

The Life of

The Wright Brothers

Emma Lynch

Heinemann
LIBRARY

www.heinemann.co.uk/library
Visit our website to find out more information about **Heinemann Library** books.

To order:
☎ Phone 44 (0) 1865 888066
🖹 Send a fax to 44 (0) 1865 314091
💻 Visit the Heinemann Bookshop at www.heinemann.co.uk/library to browse our catalogue and order online.

First published in Great Britain by Heinemann Library, Halley Court, Jordan Hill, Oxford OX2 8EJ, part of Harcourt Education.
Heinemann is a registered trademark of Harcourt Education Ltd.

Editorial: Lucy Thunder and Harriet Milles
Design: Richard Parker and
       Tinstar Design Ltd (www.tinstar.co.uk)
Picture Research: Melissa Allison and Fiona Orbell
Production: Camilla Smith

Originated by Repro Multi-Warna
Printed and bound in China by
    South China Printing Company

The paper used to print this book comes from sustainable resources.

ISBN 0 431 18097 0 (hardback)
09 08 07 06 05
10 9 8 7 6 5 4 3 2 1

ISBN 0 431 18157 8 (paperback)
10 09 08 07 06
10 9 8 7 6 5 4 3 2 1

British Library Cataloguing in Publication Data
Emma Lynch
The Wright Brothers. – (The Life of)
629.1'3'00922
A full catalogue record for this book is available from the British Library.

Acknowledgements
The Publishers would like to thank the following for permission to reproduce photographs:
p. **4** Science Photo Library/Photo Researchers;
p. **5** US Air Force; pp. **6**, **8**, **10**, **11**, **13**, **16**, **17**, **18** Special Collection and Archives, Wright State University; p. **7** Harcourt Education Ltd; p. **9** Corbis/Underwood & Underwood; p. **12** Mary Evans Picture Library; p. **15** Corbis; p. **19** Corbis/Bettmann; p. **20** Vintage Views; p. **21** Roy Nagl; pp. **14**, **22** Roger Wade Walker/Harcourt Education Ltd.; p. **23** Corbis/David Muench; pp. **24** (left), **25** (left), **25** (right) Corbis/Royalty-Free; p. **24** (right) Getty/Photodisc; p. **26** Science Photo Library/NASA; p. **27** Chris Honeywell/Harcourt Education Ltd.

Cover photograph of The Wright Brothers, reproduced with permission of Corbis/Underwood & Underwood. Page icons: Hemera PhotoObjects.

The Publishers would like to thank Rebecca Vickers for her assistance in the preparation of this book.

Every effort has been made to contact copyright holders of any material reproduced in this book. Any omissions will be rectified in subsequent printings if notice is given to the Publishers.

The Wright Brothers changed the way we see the world. These days, we can travel right across the world in a short time. This is because of their work.

Even the most modern aeroplanes work in the same way as the Wright Brothers' first plane.

An exciting present

Wilbur and Orville lived in the United States of America. Their parents were Milton and Susan Wright. Milton was a **bishop**. He often had to work away from home.

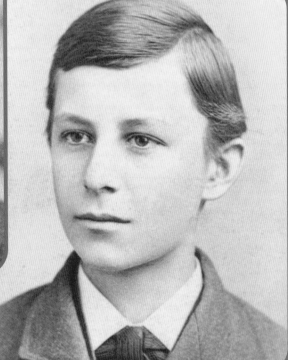

This is Wilbur (right) and Orville (left) when they were young boys.

In 1878, Milton brought home a flying toy. A rubber band made it fly. Wilbur and Orville wanted to understand how it worked. They made their own copies of it.

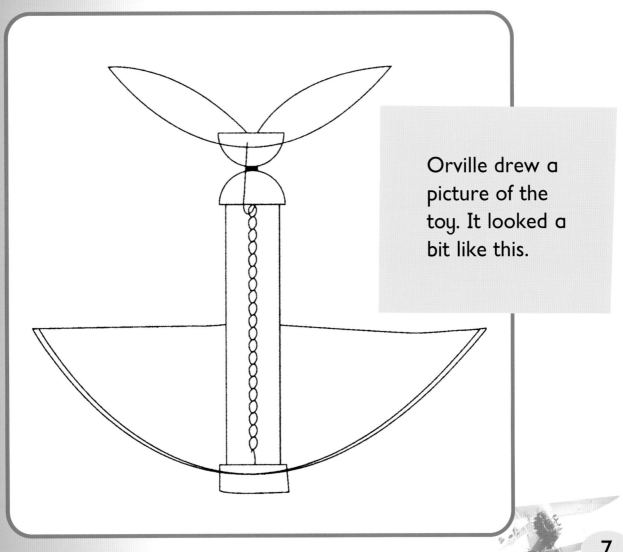

Orville drew a picture of the toy. It looked a bit like this.

The Wright Cycle Company

In 1884, the Wright family moved
to this house in Dayton, Ohio, USA.

When Wilbur left school, he decided not
to go to college. He stayed at home in
Dayton, Ohio. Orville left school and
learned to be a **printer**.

Orville opened a print shop. Wilbur went to work with him in 1890. Two years later, the brothers opened another shop. They mended and sold bicycles.

In 1896, Wilbur and Orville began to make their own bicycles to sell in their shop.

Inventing the aeroplane

By 1896, **inventors** were trying to build flying machines. The brothers **designed** an aircraft with **controls**. It could be moved around in the air, like a bike on a road.

The brothers tested their aircraft on the beaches at Kitty Hawk, North Carolina.

Wilbur and Orville tested their controls with a kite. Then they tried them with different **gliders**. They tried for several years. At last the controls worked in 1902.

The third glider became the first aircraft that could be **controlled**.

The first real aeroplane

The brothers **designed** and built a new **powered** aeroplane, called *Flyer 1*. *Flyer 1* made four short flights at Kitty Hawk on 17 December 1903.

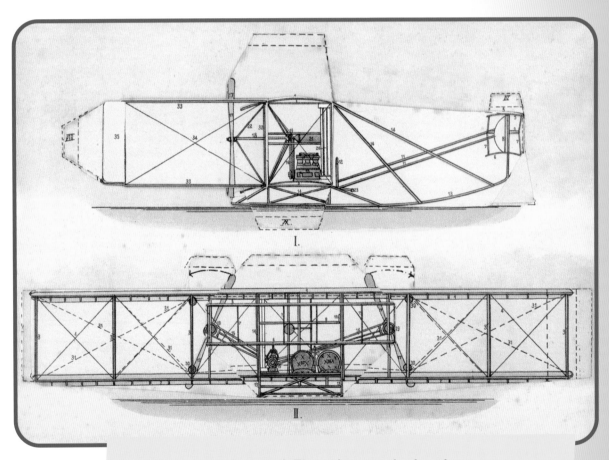

The **engine** of *Flyer 1* was light, but powerful enough to move an aeroplane.

Flyer 2 was very difficult to **control**. By 1905, the brothers could fly figures of eight in *Flyer 3*. They could stay in the air for over half an hour, and land safely.

The 1905 Wright *Flyer 3* was the first real aeroplane.

Selling the idea

The brothers tried to sell their flying machine. At last, in 1907, the US Army asked for an aeroplane. The next year, some people in France asked for one, too.

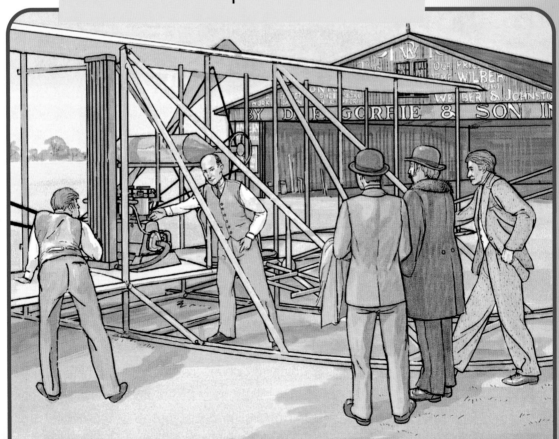

More and more people wanted to buy the Wright Brothers' aeroplanes.

The brothers made changes to *Flyer 3*. Now it could carry two people.

People wanted planes that could carry a passenger as well as a pilot. The brothers made some changes to *Flyer 3*. They tested them in secret.

Becoming famous

In 1908 and 1909, Wilbur showed Wright aircraft in Europe. Orville did show flights in Virginia, USA. One of Orville's flights ended badly, when a **propeller** fell off.

Orville's passenger was killed in the accident.

In 1909 Wilbur flew in front of one million people over New York harbour. The world was amazed by the brothers' flights. The Wright Brothers became famous.

Wilbur's test flights broke all the records. No one had ever flown so well before.

Factories and flying schools

Now more and more people wanted aeroplanes. The brothers started factories and flying schools in Europe and the USA. In 1909, they set up the Wright Company.

This man is painting a new **propeller** in the Wright Factory at Dayton, Ohio.

Most of the brothers' money still came from flying shows. The crowds wanted to see amazing and dangerous **stunts**. Soon there were more and more accidents.

The pilots had to fly fast and high to please the crowds.

Too many fights

Other people in Europe and the USA started to copy the Wright's aeroplanes. Wilbur and Orville had many fights with them. This made them very unpopular.

Glenn Curtiss, of San Diego, USA, also built early aeroplanes. The Wright Brothers had their biggest fight with him.

The brothers spent too much time fighting with people. They did not spend time making their planes better. Other people started to make better planes.

By 1911, Glenn Curtiss had made a hydroplane. It could take off and land on water!

Later years

In 1912, Wilbur died of an illness called **typhoid**. He was 45 years old. Orville did not want to work with aeroplanes any more. He sold the Wright Company.

Orville sold the Wright Company in 1916. He became an inventor again.

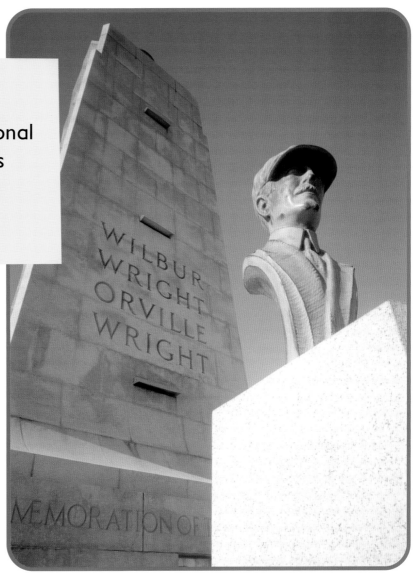

The Wright Brothers' National **Memorial** was built near Kitty Hawk.

Orville worked on his inventions in West Dayton. He also helped other **inventors** with their ideas. Orville died in 1948. He was 76 years old.

Why are the Wright Brothers famous?

The Wright Brothers' work is still important today. The **controls** they **invented** are used in modern aeroplanes, spacecraft, submarines, and even robots!

The Wright Brothers made high-speed travel possible in the world above, below and around us. They have made the world feel like a smaller place.

The Wright Brothers' work has helped to build each of these machines.

More about the Wright Brothers

Some **museums** and websites show sketches by the brothers and photos of their Flyers. They also have some letters and diaries written by the brothers.

This model of *Flyer I* is in the Science Museum in London.

We can visit **memorials** to the Wright Brothers. We can also listen to recordings of the brothers talking about their work.

Orville Wright wrote this book about the brothers' work.

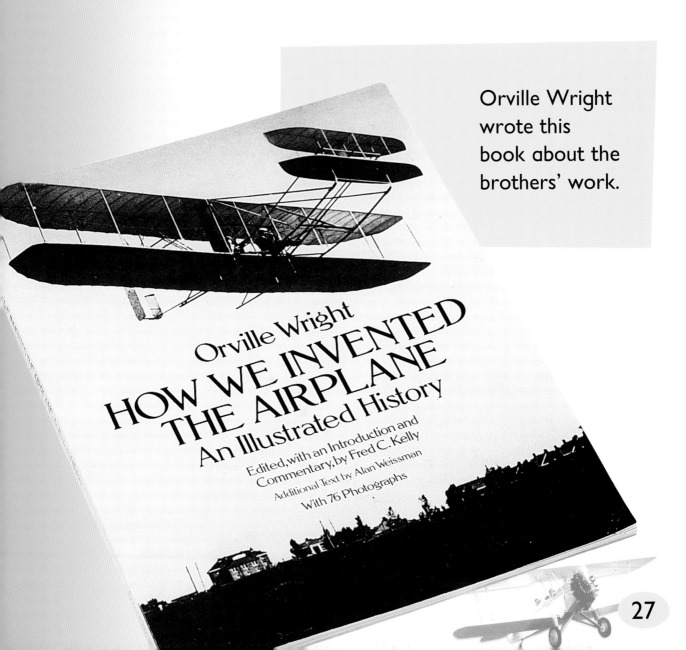

Orville Wright
HOW WE INVENTED
THE AIRPLANE
An Illustrated History
Edited, with an Introduction and
Commentary, by Fred C. Kelly
Additional Text by Alan Weissman
With 76 Photographs

 # Fact file

- An aeroplane's **controls** let it roll its wings right and left. They let it pitch (lift) its nose up and down. It can yaw (move) its nose from side to side. These were the Wright Brothers' ideas for controlling aircraft. Now all aeroplanes work in this way.

- A German man called Otto Lilienthal also made several **gliding** flights between 1891 and 1896. He even tried to fly on his own, using wings made of wood and material strapped to his arms!

- *Flyer I* is now on display at the National Air and Space Museum in Washington DC, USA.

Timeline

1867	Wilbur Wright is born on 16 April
1871	Orville Wright is born on 19 August
1878	Milton Wright brings home a flying toy **powered** by a rubber band
1896	The Wright Cycle Company begins to make bikes
1902	The Wright's third **glider** becomes the first **controllable** aircraft
1903	Flyer1, the world's first powered aeroplane, makes four short flights on 17 December
1905	Wright Flyer 3 becomes the first fully working aeroplane
1908–9	Wilbur and Orville show their Flyers in Europe and America
1912	Wilbur Wright dies on 30 May
1916	Orville sells the Wright Company
1948	Orville Wright dies on 30 January

Glossary

bishop important priest in charge of all churches in an area

design idea, often a picture, of how something will work

control way of making something work

engine machine that gives power to something to make it work

glider aeroplane with no engine

inventor someone who thinks of and makes something for the first time

memorial something to remind us of people who have died

museum place where important pieces of art or parts of history are kept

powered made to go or work using power, like an engine

printer someone who makes books or newspapers

propellers moving blades that make something push forward

stunt doing something difficult or dangerous

typhoid illness that people can die from

Find out more

Books

Into the Air: The Story of the Wright Brothers' First Flight, Robert Burleigh *et al* (Silver Whistle Books, 2002)

Great Life Stories: The Wright Brothers: Inventors of the Airplane, Bernard Ryan (Franklin Watts, 2003)

The Wright Brothers, Richard Tames (Scholastic, 1990)

Websites

http://memory.loc.gov/ammem/wrighthtml/wrighthome.html
The Library of Congress, USA. Online collection of the Wright Brothers' letters, diaries, notebooks and pictures.

http://www.first-to-fly.com/
An online museum about the Wright Brothers

Places to visit

Wright Brothers National Memorial
1401 National Park Drive, Manteo, NC 27954, USA, 001 (252) 441 7430

Index